Anima...

Why do snakes and other animals have scales?

Clare Lewis

Raintree is an imprint of Capstone Global Library Limited, a company incorporated in England and Wales having its registered office at 7 Pilgrim Street, London EC4V 6LB – Registered company number: 6695582

www.raintree.co.uk
myorders@raintree.co.uk

Edited by Clare Lewis and Kristen Mohn
Designed by Richard Parker
Picture research by Svetlana Zhurkin
Production by Victoria Fitzgerald
Originated by Capstone Global Library
Printed and bound in China by Leo Paper Products Ltd

ISBN 978 1 406 29924 3 (hardback)
19 18 17 16 15
10 9 8 7 6 5 4 3 2 1

ISBN 978 1 406 29929 8 (paperback)
20 19 18 17 16
10 9 8 7 6 5 4 3 2 1

British Library Cataloguing in Publication Data
A full catalogue record for this book is available from the British Library.

Acknowledgements
We would like to thank the following for permission to reproduce photographs: Corbis: Clouds Hill Imaging, 12 (inset); Dreamstime: Girishhc, 5 (top left), Howard Chew, 19, Jeff Moore, 5 (right), Peter Leahy, 7; Getty Images: Cosmos Blank, 20, 23; iStockphoto: photographer3431, 11; Shutterstock: Asmus, 16, Audrey Snider-Bell, cover (bottom), 17, 23, bochimsang12, 5 (bottom left), Ew Chee Guan, 23 (pest), Joe Belanger, 12 (back), Matt Jeppson, 4, 8, 22 (bottom), Matteo photos, 14, mycteria (fish scales), cover and throughout, Naypong, back cover (left), 10, 23, Oleg Shipov, 6, 22 (top right), 23, Pete Niesen, 18, 23, reptiles4all, 13, 21, Rich Carey, cover (top), SJ Allen, 15, Vlad61, back cover (right), 9, 22 (top left)

We would like to thank Michael Bright for his invaluable help in the preparation of this book.

Contents

Some words are shown in bold, **like this**. You can find them in the picture glossary on page 23.

Which animals have scales?

Most reptiles have hard, dry scales. Reptiles are **cold-blooded** animals. They lay eggs.

A snake is a type of reptile.

Fish have scales, too. Many birds have scales on their ankles and feet.

Very few mammals have scales. Pangolins are mammals with scales.

pangolin

What are scales?

Scales are a type of body covering.

Snake and other reptile scales are made from the same **material** as your fingernails and hair.

Fish scales grow out of the skin of the fish.

Some fish scales are small and smooth. Others are large and spiky.

Are scales colourful?

Reptile scales can be very colourful.

The bright colours of this coral snake warn other animals that its bite can hurt them.

Many fish are very colourful.

But the colour and patterns on fish do not come from their scales. They come from the skin underneath. Most fish scales have no colour.

How do scales protect animals?

Crocodiles have hard, bony scales on their backs. Their scales are like a suit of armour.

Snakes have thin skin. Their tough scales help to protect them from bites, bumps and scratches.

Some fish scales are smooth and covered with slippery slime. This helps fish escape from **predators**.

Can scales help animals catch their prey?

Shark scales are like tiny sharp teeth. They make shark skin feel very rough.

The scales move slightly when the shark swims. This helps the shark swim fast after its **prey**.

Wart snakes live in the water. They have
rough, pointy scales. They help the snake
to hold on to fish that it catches.

How do scales help animals move?

Snakes have large scales on their bellies. This helps them to glide along the ground.

Many fish scales are small. They often make overlapping layers.

The layers make it easy for fish to bend and move quickly from side to side.

Do some snakes have special scales?

Snakes have no eyelids. They cannot blink or close their eyes.

They have clear scales that cover their eyes. The scales protect the eyes from dirt and damage.

Rattlesnakes have special scales on their tails.

The scales rattle together and make a loud noise. This warns **predators** to keep away.

How do fish take care of their scales?

Some **pests** like to live on fish scales. They can hurt the fish.

Salmon try to knock pests off. They scrape their scales against the bottom of the riverbed.

Cleaner fish eat the dead skin and pests on bigger fish. This helps to keep the scales on the bigger fish clean.

How do snake scales grow?

As snakes grow, they get too big for their scaly skin. A layer of skin and scales comes off all at once.

This is called **moulting**. Underneath, a new layer of scales is ready.

When snakes moult, they get rid of any ticks or mites that were on their scales.

The new scales are clean and healthy.

Scales quiz

Which of these pictures shows snake scales?

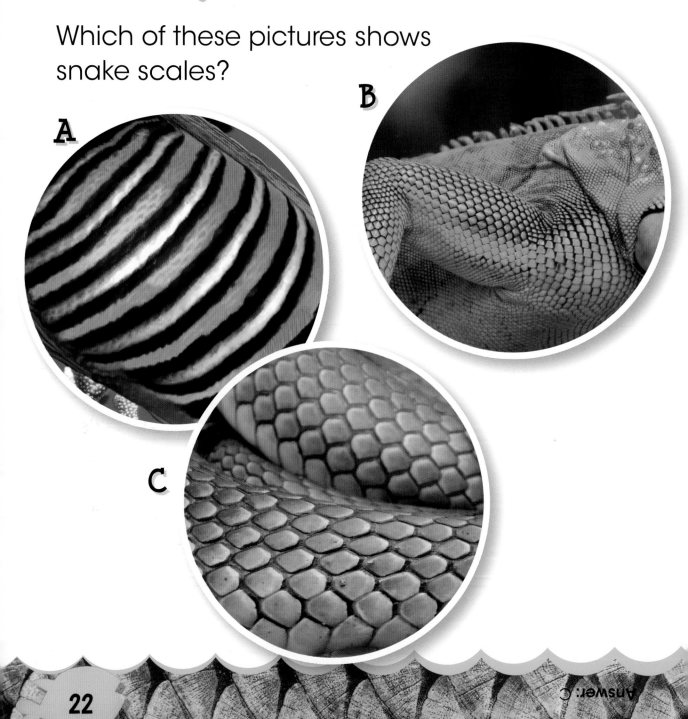

A

B

C

Answer: C

Picture glossary

 **cold-blooded** animal that cannot store its own heat in its body. Snakes and other reptiles are cold-blooded.

 **material** substance from which something is made

 **moult** to shed a layer of skin or other body covering

 **pest** tiny animal that lives on and harms a bigger animal

 **predator** animal that hunts and eats other animals

 **prey** animal that is hunted and eaten by predators

Find out more

Websites

bbc.co.uk/nature/life/Reptile
Discover reptile facts, watch videos and hear the latest news.

bbc.co.uk/nature/life/Shark
Find out more about this amazing predator of the sea.

kids.sandiegozoo.org/animals/reptiles
Discover some interesting reptiles, such as giant tortoises and venomous snakes.

Books

Focus on Fish, Stephen Savage (Wayland, 2014)

Reptiles, (Animal Classifications), Angela Royston (Raintree, 2015)

Snakes (Amazing Animals), Jen Green (Franklin Watts, 2011)

Index